Angel's Diary

Inspirational Poems

Shuchita Aggarwal

BookLeaf Publishing

India | USA | UK

Dedication

Hello avid readers. All my poems are self-written and are drawn from my own experiences and inspirations I've found in my own life and in the people around me. This book of 21 poems will be a very special book for me, and I am sure it will also inspire you in your life in some way or the other.

Acknowledgement

I would take this as an opportunity to thank BookLeaf Publishing for giving me a golden opportunity to showcase some of my poems which are very close to my heart. It's a collection of old and new poetry meant for the new age people, young and adults. Thank you to the entire team of BookLeaf Publishing who work tirelessly behind the scenes and get our books published.

Looking forward to having my copy of the book soon. Thank you to those who will be reading my poems soon.

Cheers.

Preface

My purpose behind writing these poems is to make people aware of their suppressed emotions and also help them understand themselves better. All our lives we try to comprehend other people's actions and behaviour towards us, and oftentimes many of us lose sight of ourselves in this process. This book of poetry is all about self-reflection, self-growth, and self-learning.

1. Love & Emotions!

Sometimes in Love,
Emotions run so deep......
Fiddling with the old memories,
That we retain for keeps.

Holding on to such emotions,
Is not easy for sure......
Even Science and medicine,
Fail to offer any cure.

Grief is a boat,
No one wants to board,
Those who ride on it,
Are looking for a peaceful shore.

A ray of hope,
A glimpse of light,
A rising sun,
That's oh! So bright!

Life is magical,

Don't self-sabotage it with doubts.
You have come this far,
So, now it's time to make yourself and
your parents proud.

Love yourself more today and celebrate
being YOU!

2. Unsettled Mind!

Sometimes, our mind becomes a wanderer,
It just can't relax!
It cooks stories by itself,
and keeps looking for hacks.

Some people seek external validation,
While others run towards safety.
But for those who want peace,
Find doing all this too hasty!

Some people pretend to be nice,
While others are snobbish and grey.
They will show you their true colours,
When things don't go their way!

Some people are judgemental,
While some think too much.
Some people just shy away,
Their personality is such.

However you are,
Be true to yourself.
Self-reflect and grow,

And be what you want to be,
Feel calm and relaxed,
As we all have some bad days.
Don't you worry,
That's what the universe says!

Universe always has our back!

3. Me And My Heart!

Knock Knock!
Who is this?
I am your heart,
And I am connected to your soul.
And You and I are never apart.

But then why does it hurt so much,
When we are grieving a loss?
Why can't we stop the tears,
If we are our own boss!

Heart says,
I am just a feeling,
that resides deep within you.
I always replenish and grow,
And want to see you anew.

I would never want you to be sad,
If that happens,
It's my bad.

Open me up,
As it's a brand new day —

A day filled with laughter and joy,
Should keep you at bay!

Never lose me from your sight,
As I am your breathing space.
Always know that you are special,
And I am here to stay.

Yours Truly,
Your Heart.

keep your heart safe as it is very precious!

4. Your Life, Your Motto!

Focus on your goals,
Don't let anyone bog you down.
You are your own strength,
Always remember that....
So reverse that frown!

Sometimes we wonder,
Why people behave as such.
But to be honest,
Now it doesn't bother me much.

Life has many phases,
Universe teaches us a lot.
Your thoughts are powerful,
Reminding you....
If you just forgot.

We can say,
Sometimes life is mysterious,
It brings us what we asked.
Still we try to figure out,
If the situation is going to last.

Happy times or bad,
Never lose your grace.
Always believe in the good,
As you are under universe's warm embrace.

What's your life's motto?

5. Emotional Check!

We all are humans,
And we express ourselves through various
emotions.
Sometimes we feel well-contained within our
own safe shell,
Other times our emotions are scattered
everywhere as we repel.
Nearing the end of this year, let's feel some
merriment and cheer.

Happy moments, whether from past or
present,
Let's be grateful for all that exists.
Dwelling in the past,
Will only hold you back from your upcoming
future.
So weigh your decisions as you heal and grow,
For what future holds for you,
You never know.

We all can feel bogged down,

We all can feel the highs and the lows.
But eventually my friends,
Feelings can't be held back for too long.

Our heart often struggles,
And wants quick resolutions.
But our mind wants to stop and think,
Is it the right solution?

keep your emotions in check.

6. Friendships!

A friend is someone,
Who doesn't belittle.
Who wants the best for you,
And with you, would be subtle.

As you nurture your connection,
It will become strong.
With doubts and mind-games,
It won't stay for long.

True friends are like diamonds,
A very rare find.
To retain and keep them,
Sometimes we have to be extra kind.

Genuine ones won't leave you,
No matter what you say or do.
Because they know your heart,
And they know the real you.

You might have them out of your sight,
Sometimes you may even end up in a fight.
But if the connection is pure,
And the intentions are right,
They will find the way back,
And hug you tight.

True friend(s) understand,
Your frown behind that smile.
To set things right,
They will travel an extra mile.

Hold onto such friends,
As they are very dear.
In our mundane lives,
They bring glory and cheer.

Do you have any special friend(s) in your life?
If yes, you are blessed.

7. Let the nature heal you today!

We have beautiful flowers,
In various hues.
Brilliant red,
And sunny yellow too.

Red expresses desires, joy & love,
Orange adds to the brightness & spark.
Yellow can ignite new friendships,
And Pink represents success after hardships.

Roses have meanings too.....
Orange rose stands for passion,
White rose depicts purity.
Red rose brings true love,
That needs to be dealt with maturity.

Blue rose brings mystery,
Black rose symbolizes new beginnings &
death.
Pink rose brings gratitude,

That we shouldn't stop until our last breath.
Let's learn from nature,
Let's try to understand life.
We can't be happy forever,
But that's what we all strive.

Nature is a magical healer. Heal your heart
and mind.

8. You are your own lighthouse.

Whenever you are feeling lost,
Whenever your heart wanders,
Whenever your mind is dwindling,
All you want is a lighthouse.

It will ignite a ray of hope,
So don't give up on you, my friend,
For you still have a lot of scope.

When you are filled with gratitude,
All you need is some solitude.
I would say, don't give up on you,
As all days are not the same,
On sunny days too, we see rain.

When you are feeling oh so stuck,
And your head is filled with multiple
thoughts,
Just wait and relax, don't give up on you,

Because you are special and unique,
And you are one of a kind,
Irreplaceable child of god.

Don't give up on yourself ever.....

9. Nurture the bond of friendship.

We all are searching for true friends,
We share a different bond with everyone.
You may like someone for their wit,
Or you might like them, for they keep
themself fit.

You might like them for the way they dress,
Or you might like them as they know how to
impress.
You can like someone for how they care,
Or for being friendly and fair.

Sometimes you feel the warmth around them,
And you feel safe.
You may lean on them,
And maybe cry on their shoulder.
You know the other person won't judge you,

And with them, you won't even notice when
night will turn to dawn.

You might like someone for that cheerful
smile,
But you still may never know,
They can themselves be sad,
But being happy is just their style.

You might pick a friend for so many reasons,
But never make friendships for a purpose,
As those are short-lived,
Only make friends with pure heart and
intentions,
Even if distance separates you,
True friendship knows no dimensions.

Nurture the bond of friendship within your
connections.

10. Little joys of life.

We try our hardest,
When the sea is rough.
Trying to find solutions,
In situations that are tough.

Things are no longer the same,
They never will be.
It does make me sad at times,
But I draw an inner strength,
From the sources that are unknown,
That are unseen.

These hidden divine forces help me move
ahead,
With courage and dedication,
Longing to do something,
And come up with new creations.

As some things can't be reversed.
Like our age or our existence on this planet.
Worrying is just going to add to the stress,

So relax and let go!
Feel elated and kick the lows.

I know it's easier said than done,
We all are chasing something,
As if always on the run.

For once, let's be playful,
Once in a while find yourself.
Don't pretend to be someone else,
And follow your heart.
Fill your life with simple joys,
Let the universe fill your cart.

Follow the mantra: To always look ahead in
life.

11. Source of light.

I perceive life in a different way,
Finding the light from within.
Sometimes I try to meditate,
Under the sun's bright sheen.

As the sun sets,
We have the moon to ponder on.
And when the moonlight gets dim,
Or it plays a game of hide-and-seek,
We sit back,
Searching for the light that exists within.

When our heart and mind are aligned,
When we stand in our own power,
When even to the life's bitter truth,
We are no longer blind.
When we are not artificial,
When we make the right choices for
ourselves,
That are not superficial.

Still having a hopeful heart,
Almighty wrote my life's destiny,
From the time I was born.
I should have known this from the start.

Be your own source of light. Talk to the stars,
moon, and the sun.

12. Count your blessings!

We say,
Eyes are fascinating,
As they possess to express what's unsaid.
When your eyes are wet,
And you know the reason why,
All you really want,
Is a lonely place to cry.

But you can't complain much,
Neither can you sulk,
For along with these emotions,
Worries come in bulk.

People are quick to judge,
Mock and form opinions.
Life feels so fizzled,
As we fear and ponder too much.

Now as I change my perception,
And I count my blessings more,
My anxiety dissipates,

Which works wonders for my future growth.

Count your blessings more than the number
of friends that you are able to make. Connect
with the universe.

13. All about loving someone.

When we say,
We are in love....
When we say,
We can see the white doves.

Symbol of peace and love,
Oh! So pure and divine,
One can only love when the heart is pure,
Manipulations and mind games don't give any cure.

Self-doubts and fears play their part too....
Especially when the love connection is new.
But once the trust is built,
And the foundation becomes strong,
No one can break it,
If the intentions are not wrong.

Never take shortcuts in love,
Be authentic and strong.
However if things don't work out,
Don't panic, don't frown.

Life is still beautiful,
Don't close your heart to new love.
Sometimes it's the god's way of giving you the
best,
So surrender to the divine and be at rest.

Did you ever love someone who betrayed you?
Forgive and forget, and move ahead with your
head held high.

14. What is life?

I never knew before,
How it felt to be heavy around the heart.
I feel, we can compare our lives,
To a shopping cart.

We fill it with all things fancy and nice,
It makes us happy,
We feel suffice.
If we don't get what's on the list,
We clutch our fists.

Each time we go shopping,
We pick up different items,
Just like in life....
Sometimes we get sadness,
Next moment we have hope,
Sometimes our faith is strong,
Other times we have tougher situations to
cope (still having faith)

At times it takes a lifetime,
To understand LIFE.
And sometimes we get its true essence,
In the blink of an eye.

Sometimes we are so lost,
We demand solitude,
Sometimes we get universal messages and
blessings,
Which help us reach abundance and good
fortune.

Do you download the messages which
universe shows you in magical ways? Such as a
song or a phrase you come across!

15. Sunshine!

When sun shines on you,
When you welcome a day that's new.
When you know you are right,
Your days seem nice and bright.

No competitions and nothing to explain,
You find your mind peaceful and sane.
Fame, glory, and abundance all exist within you,
So create a beautiful symphony that's long overdue.

Not shifting from your goals,
Side by side working on your soul,
Moving on the right path,
You will find your true role.

Don't let anyone bog you down,
For they don't know your heart.
So always keep moving forward,
And fill your life-cart.

Are you shining as bright as the sun? Or you have some sunshine in your life.... :)

16. Grief!

A small five-letter word: Grief....
It weighs too heavily.
No one wants to face it,
It's not something everyone can handle.

When days are long,
Nights seem even longer.
You have wept enough,
Until universe prepares you to be stronger.

When you put on that brave face,
People watch you in awe.
Seldom do they know,
All that you saw.

Gratitude and manifestations help a lot,
That's my personal experience.
Constant healing is called for,
And you have to open your heart.

You become empathetic towards others,
As if you can feel their loss.
You too have gone through some tough days,
Your emotions make you so gross.

Always be brave,
Don't lose yourself ever.
Keep healing and growing,
As you reach victories that you will savour.

Grief is a boat that no one wants to ride. So
ride on it alone and win your battles.

17. Breakups

Breakups are hurtful,
Sometimes even spiteful.
Full of regrets,
A lot remains unsaid.

Your heart feels pain,
As if in tears,
Inflicting doubts and lots of fears.
Sometimes love leaves you devastated,
And you may feel oh so lost,
Not knowing losing such relationships would
come at such a heavy cost.

Every situation may not be so bad,
With your positive mindset,
You can become happy from sad.
Do some self-care and self-love,
Because life is beautiful,
No matter what, you have to keep yourself
cheerful.

Still try to be understanding and kind,
As you live for yourself,
Unfold your blinds.
Don't hurt anyone in the process,
As karma is real.

Universe is fair enough,
And shall give you what you reap.
Today is a new day,
So awaken yourself and think deep.

Have you gone through a breakup or dealt
with one which didn't feel like a fair ending?

18. Gratitude & Trust....

Walking down the memory lane,
Today I paused a little.
Overwhelming thoughts pondered over me,
Making me feel so puzzled.

Trusting on my inner self —
My guide and my soul strength,
I refused to give up,
And emerge even stronger than before.
I never knew I possessed so much of strength,
Which I had kept hidden for sure.

Gratitude played the ball game in my life,
It changed everything for me,
It brought me a lot of smiles.

I learnt to accept situations,
Thanking everything that came my way.
Even if it was a lesson from the divine, I took
it as a learning,
Letting the universe have its say.

I thank everyone,
Who came into my life for a reason.
I even thank those,
Who stayed with me for a few seasons.

I feel myself abundantly blessed,
As I align myself with the universe.
only thinking about the positives,
Curbing away all the curse.
Thanking the divine,
Creating a beautiful life, which I can call
mine.

Be happy, be blessed.

19. Hope you have not forgotten...

I am thankful for this life,
It teaches me a lot.
It keeps me grounded in reality,
As I reassure myself, all my thoughts.

Hope you don't forget, to say "Thank you."
Hope you don't forget, to smile at a day that's new.
Hope you don't forget, you have lots of things to do.
Hope you don't forget, that all the power lies within you.

Hope you don't forget,
You are meant to rise and shine.
Hope you don't forget,
Sometimes you have to create a strong boundary line.

Hoping and wishing for the very best,
Keeping emotions in control,
As we continue to live our lives,
Each of us play our unique roles.

Hope you are not forgetting something today
that you left unsaid or undone!!

20. Because You Are Most Important

Give love in abundance,
Be kind and nurturing.
Don't forget to fill your reservoir,
Be strong,
Be a survivor.

Fight for your rights,
Don't accept if things are wrong.
You deserve the very best,
So sing a happy song.

Treat everyone with humbleness,
But don't become a doormat.
For you are most important,
So stay away from brats.

Love yourself the most today,
As that's the best you can do.

Hoping for the good always,
As you feel excited for the phase in your life
that's new.

Never look back,
At those, who hurt you.
Because they were never meant to be.
So hug yourself today,
For being a transformed YOU.

A new you, that was created by learnings,
lessons and people's attitude towards you.

21. Take life easy.

Sipping my morning cup of tea,
Feeling the cool breeze.
Letting the nature heal me,
As I feel more at ease.

Toxicity leaving my surroundings,
As I feel more at ease.
I let myself be elevated,
As positive thoughts, I don't dismiss.

Forgiving and learning,
As I nurture and grow.
Surrendering to the divine,
I find my true self-worth on the go.

Nature works at its best,
When you let it work by itself.
So don't force and don't stress,
Abundance and blessings are coming your
way,

So open your heart and don't suppress.

As you take your life easy,
You start feeling relaxed.
Tensions dissipate,
And opportunities surface.

Mantra to follow in life: The policy of taking
it easy.